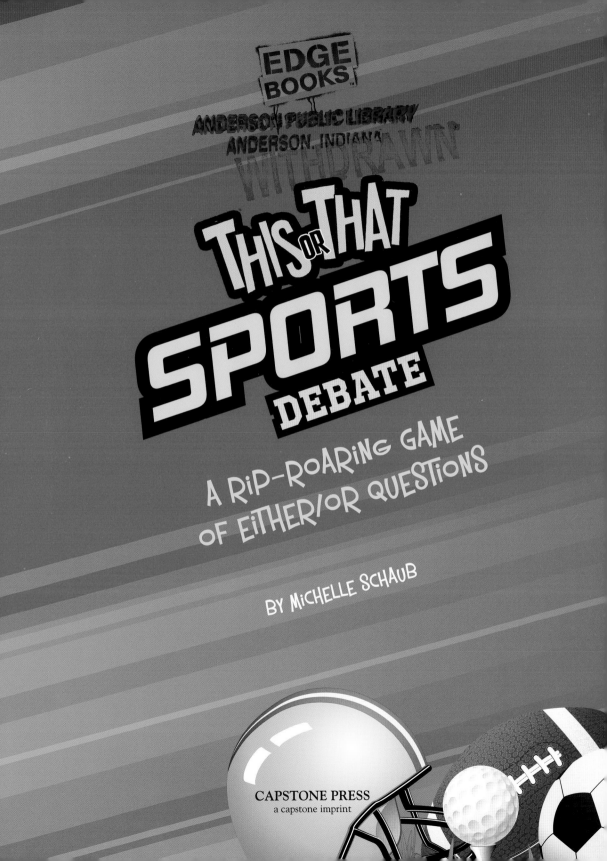

EDGE BOOKS

THIS OR THAT

SPORTS

DEBATE

A RIP-ROARING GAME
OF EITHER/OR QUESTIONS

BY MICHELLE SCHAUB

CAPSTONE PRESS
a capstone imprint

Edge Books are published by Capstone Press,
1710 Roe Crest Drive, North Mankato, Minnesota 56003.
www.capstonepub.com

Library of Congress Cataloging-in-Publication Data
Schaub, Michelle.
 This or that sports debate : a rip-roaring game of either or questions /
   by Michelle Schaub.
   p. cm.—(Edge books : this or that?)
 Includes bibliographical references and index.
 Summary: "Offers intriguing either/or questions and content on sports topics
   to encourage critical thinking and debate"—Provided by publisher.
 ISBN 978-1-4296-8592-4 (library binding)
 ISBN 978-1-4296-9276-2 (paperback)
 ISBN 978-1-62065-236-7 (ebook PDF)
 1. Sports—Miscellanea—Juvenile literature. I. Title.
 GV705.4.S37 2013
 796—dc23   2011053148

Editorial Credits
Anthony Wacholtz, editor; Veronica Correia, designer; Eric Gohl, media researcher;
   Laura Manthe, production specialist

Image Credits
AP Images: Nick Wass, 13; BigStockPhoto: Andrew Kazmierski, 20; Corbis:
Bettmann, 26, 27; Dreamstime: Fairwayphotos, 8, Grosremy, 19, Jerry Coli, 7,
Madookaboo, 16, Rick Sargeant, 29, Sarah Dusautoir, 18, Scott Anderson, 5, Todd
Taulman, 6; Newscom: Icon SMI/John Cordes, 25, Icon SMI/Tom Croke, 17, MCT/
Ron Jenkins, 4, Paul Buck, 24, Reuters/Gary Caskey, 28, Thomas Eisenhuth, 22;
Shutterstock: Aspen Photo, 2–3, 14, Christopher Penler, 21, chwl, cover (top left),
Debby Wong, 15, Diagon, 1, 32, Ffooter, 9, Jose Carvalho, cover (bottom
right), Keo, cover (design element), Kirk Geisler, 11, Left Eyed
Photography, 23, Lukich, 12, Marc Pagani Photography,
10, prudkov, cover (design element)

Printed in the United States of America in
Stevens Point, Wisconsin.
032012   006678WZF12

All statistics are through 2011.

HOW TO USE THIS BOOK:

Have you ever dreamed of dodging tackles like Devin Hester? Serving tennis balls like Serena Williams? Swimming like Michael Phelps? But if you had to pick, which would you choose?

This book presents questions that ask you to choose between two different sports situations. Use reasoning and imagination to choose the best option. While you're at it, you'll learn fun facts about some of the greatest teams, athletes, and historic moments in sports.

PLAY ONE-ON-ONE AGAINST

LEBRON JAMES

- forward for the Miami Heat
- 6 feet, 8 inches (203 centimeters) tall; 250 pounds (113 kilograms)
- 27.7 career points per game

LeBron James has been a dominant player ever since he joined the National Basketball Association (NBA). He was picked first in the 2003 NBA draft by the Cleveland Cavaliers. James' powerful dunks, quick moves, and all-around amazing play earned him NBA MVP awards in 2009 and 2010. The seven-time All-Star led the Miami Heat to the NBA Finals in 2011.

COVER
LARRY FITZGERALD

- wide receiver for the Arizona Cardinals
- 6 feet, 3 inches (191 cm) tall; 218 lbs (99 kg)
- career touchdowns: 73

Larry Fitzgerald was the third pick in the 2004 NFL draft by the Arizona Cardinals. He is the first player in team history to score at least 10 touchdowns in three straight seasons. He has incredible body control, making him difficult to cover. The wide receiver's lanky body, jumping ability, and great hands have earned him five Pro Bowl appearances. He knows just how to position himself to make the perfect touchdown catch.

THIS

AROLDIS CHAPMAN

54

GET HIT BY A MAJOR-LEAGUE PITCHER'S FASTBALL?

- most common pitch in baseball
- reaches speeds of 100 miles per hour (mph) or more
- easiest pitch for most pitchers to control

Also known as smoke, gas, dead red, and express, the fastball has been blazing through strike zones since the 1880s. Today's pro baseball pitchers can really throw the heat. In 2010 Aroldis Chapman set the Major League Baseball (MLB) record for fastest pitch. The radar gun showed 105.1 mph from Chapman's scorching fastball. Although most pitchers can't top 100 mph, the fastball can still be dangerous. Many batters have been bruised by the speedy pitch. More serious injuries have ranged from concussions and lost teeth to shattered cheekbones. In the early 1900s, two players died after getting hit in the head by a pitch.

OR THAT?

GET HIT BY A
PRO HOCKEY PLAYER'S SLAP SHOT

- hardest shot in hockey
- reaches speeds of 100 miles (161 kilometers) per hour or more
- less accurate than other hockey shots

Bernard "Boom Boom" Geoffrion of the Montreal Canadiens made the slap shot popular in the 1950s. Already a powerful shot then, the slap shot is even more fearsome today. During a skills competition in 2012, Zdeno Chara set the National Hockey League (NHL) record for fastest slap shot at 108.8 miles (175 km) per hour. Shots that powerful can really do some damage. In 2009 Philadelphia Flyers center Ian Laperriere got hit in the face with a slap shot. The result? Seven missing teeth and 100 stitches.

ZDENO CHARA

THIS

WiN THE MASTERS

- one of the four major championships in professional golf
- top players: Jack Nicklaus, Arnold Palmer, Tiger Woods, Phil Mickelson
- 2011 winner prize money: $1.44 million

The Masters is held every April at Augusta National Golf Club in Augusta, Georgia. About 100 of the best golfers in the world are invited to compete in this high-status contest that started in 1934. The winner is awarded the green jacket. Charl Schwartzel, the 2011 winner, brought home $1.44 million. But you don't have to take first to earn some money. The 20th-place winner in 2011 earned $104,000.

OR THAT?

WIN THE U.S. OPEN

- one of the four major tournaments in professional tennis
- top players: Pete Sampras, Roger Federer, Steffi Graf, Martina Navratilova
- 2011 prize money for winner of singles (men and women): $1.8 million

Every August more than 600 of the best athletes in tennis gather in Queens, New York, for the U.S. Open. Players battle it out on the courts of the United States Tennis Association (USTA) Billie Jean King National Tennis Center. The tournament was first held in 1881 and is divided into five events: men's and women's singles, men's and women's doubles, and mixed doubles. A player can become a Grand Slam winner by taking first in all four pro tournaments in a single year.

THIS

TOUR DE FRANCE

- 2,090- to 3,000-mile (3,360- to 4,830-km) bicycle race through France and surrounding countries
- 21 riding days and two rest days
- cyclists ride up to six hours a day

The Tour de France is considered the biggest test of endurance of all sports. Cyclists race thousands of miles while reaching speeds of 70 miles (113 km) per hour downhill. They can burn up to 10,000 calories a day. To stay energized, cyclists must refuel often, but there's no time to stop for a picnic. Instead, riders grab feed bags from crew members standing along the roadside. The bags hold energy snacks that the cyclists munch on as they zip along. Talk about fast food!

OR THAT?

ENDURE THE
IDITAROD

- a sled dog race in Alaska stretching 1,150 miles (1,850 km) from Anchorage to Nome
- 10 to 17 days total
- teams can race more than 11 hours a day

The Iditarod has been called the "Last Great Race on Earth." Sled teams are made up of 12 to 16 dogs and their musher. The teams must brave frozen rivers, blinding winds, and sub-zero temperatures. After long days of skimming across the brutal yet breathtaking Alaskan landscape, teams stop at checkpoints. Mushers spend this "rest" time repairing equipment and caring for the dogs. After a quick snooze, it's back to the trail. The sled team that crosses the finish line first gets a cash prize, but all teams that finish are considered winners.

THIS

SERVE LIKE
SERENA WILLIAMS

- has won two Olympic gold medals for women's doubles
- has earned 27 Grand Slam titles
- serve can reach speeds of 125 miles (201 km) per hour

Serena Williams is considered by many to be one of the greatest women's tennis players of all time. Opponents often have difficulty returning her ferocious serve. During the 2010 Wimbledon Championship, Williams fired a record 89 aces over seven matches. Her lightning strike has really paid off. As of 2011, she has earned more prize money in her career than any other female athlete in history.

OR THAT?

SHOOT LIKE MAYA MOORE

- star forward for the Minnesota Lynx
- won 2010 Excellence in Sports Performance Yearly (ESPY) Award for Best Female College Athlete
- averaged 19.7 points per game in her collegiate career

Maya Moore is no stranger to victory. During college, she led the University of Connecticut to two National Championships and a record 90-game winning streak. She became the all-time leading scorer for the University of Connecticut with 3,036 points. In 2011 Moore was picked first in the Women's National Basketball Association (WNBA) draft. The 6-foot (183-cm) forward averaged an impressive 13.2 points per game in her first season with the Minnesota Lynx.

ROY HALLADAY

PITCH A
PERFECT GAME

- factors: pitcher's skill, fielders' skills, luck
- odds: MLB season has 2,430 total games; a perfect game occurs on average once every 10 years
- 20 perfect games in MLB history out of more than 200,000 games

A perfect game is one of the rarest events in sports. More people have circled the moon than pitched a perfect game in the MLB. To perform this feat, a pitcher cannot allow any hits or walks. He can't hit any batters, and his teammates cannot have any errors. Not one opposing player can reach first base. No one pitched a perfect game from 1922 to 1956, but it happened twice in 2010. Dallas Braden of the Oakland Athletics earned a perfect game against the Tampa Bay Rays on May 9, 2010. Philadelphia Phillies ace Roy Halladay fired a perfect game against the Florida Marlins just 20 days later.

OR THAT?

SHOOT A HOLE IN ONE

- factors: golfer's skill, length of hole, luck
- odds: on a par 3 hole, about 1 in 2,500 for a pro golfer
- Andrew Magee is the only pro golfer in history to hit a hole in one on a par 4

A hole in one, or an ace, occurs when a golfer hits the ball from the tee and into the cup with one shot. Some players are aces at making aces. Jack Nicklaus scored 20 aces in his professional golf career. Tiger Woods has 18 as of 2011. Kathy Whitworth tops the Ladies Professional Golf Association (LPGA) with 11. But you don't need to be a pro to chase the ace. The odds of an amateur sinking a hole in one on a par 3? About one in 12,500.

TIGER WOODS

PEYTON MANNING

- quarterback for the Indianapolis Colts since 1998
- percentage of passes completed: 64.9
- most passing yards in a season: 4,700

Since being drafted first in 1998, Peyton Manning has been at the top of the quarterback class. He threw for more than 3,000 yards in 13 consecutive seasons. He holds the record for most NFL MVP awards with four. In 2007 Manning led the Colts to a Super Bowl victory over the Chicago Bears. Football is in his blood. He is the son of former NFL quarterback Archie Manning and brother of Eli, the New York Giants quarterback.

OR THAT?

TOM BRADY

- quarterback with the New England Patriots since 2000
- percentage of passes completed: 63.8
- most passing yards in a season: 5,235

Tom Brady may be the best NFL draft steal in history. He was the 199th pick of the 2000 draft. Despite the late selection, Brady proved to be a star quarterback. He threw for more than 3,500 yards in six straight seasons. In 2007 he threw 50 touchdown passes, breaking the NFL single-season record. Brady's no stranger to the playoffs. He has led the Patriots to three Super Bowl victories.

THIS

MICHAEL PHELPS

- won eight Olympic gold medals in 2008
- has set world records in the 100-meter and 200-meter butterfly
- has completed the 100-meter butterfly, 100-meter freestyle, and 100-meter backstroke in under 51 seconds each

Michael Phelps was built to swim. His long body is like the hull of a ship. His massive hands and feet are like paddles. His mighty kick propels him through the water like a torpedo. Since his first Olympic appearance in 2000, Phelps has shattered records. He collected eight gold medals in the 2008 Olympics, the most any athlete has earned in a single Olympics. Phelps' fame doesn't come without hard work. He swims at least 50 miles (80 kilometers) a week during his peak training.

OR THAT?

RUN LIKE USAIN BOLT

- won three Olympic gold medals in 2008
- has set world records in the 100-meter and 200-meter dash
- runs 100 meters in less than 10 seconds

At 6 feet, 5 inches (196 cm), Usain Bolt towers over other sprinters. He flashes down the track with electric energy. No wonder some fans call him Lightning Bolt. At the 2009 World Championships, Bolt lived up to his nickname. He scorched the record books with a 100-meter time of 9.58 seconds. To stay up to speed, Bolt trains up to five hours a day.

THIS

BE PART OF THE NEW YORK YANKEES FRANCHISE

- 27 World Series championships
- 43 players in Baseball Hall of Fame
- Yankees legends: Babe Ruth, Lou Gehrig, Mickey Mantle, Derek Jeter

Since the team became the Yankees in 1913, the New York franchise has been a dominant MLB team. They have won more championships than any other pro sports team in history. In baseball alone, the St. Louis Cardinals claim a distant second with 11 World Series wins. With so many baseball legends wearing the Yankees' pinstripes, it's easy to see how this team became a dynasty. Although there is a lot to cheer about, being a fan of the Bronx Bombers can be tough. There is a widespread fan base that cheers against the Yankees as well.

OR THAT?

BE PART OF THE BOSTON CELTICS FRANCHISE

- 17 NBA championships
- 25 players in the Basketball Hall of Fame
- Celtics legends: Bill Russell, Larry Bird, Robert Parish, John Havlicek, Bob Cousy

The Boston Celtics began pounding the basketball court in 1946. They started to hit their prime in the late 1950s. From 1957 to 1969, the Celtics nabbed 11 NBA championships. After two more title wins in the 1970s and three in the 1980s, the Celtics hit a lull. But in 2007 the Celtics' magic was back after trading for Kevin Garnett and Ray Allen. Along with Paul Pierce, the "Big Three" dominated the court for a 2007–2008 NBA championship win.

ABBY WAMBACH

- full-time player on U.S. Women's National Team since 2003
- 13 World Cup goals
- has earned the U.S. Soccer organization's honor of U.S. Female Soccer Athlete of the Year four times

When Abby Wambach plays soccer, she really uses her head. The forward holds the record for the most goals per game in U.S. history. More than a third of the goals have been headers. She watches the ball like a hawk and knows just how to time her jumps. Wambach used her signature move to tie Brazil during the 2011 World Cup, and the United States went on to win.

OR THAT?

DAVID BECKHAM

- pro soccer player since 1995
- 60 career goals
- won the ESPY Award for Best Major League Soccer (MLS) Player in 2008

David Beckham is a master of the free kick. The English soccer player has an amazing ability to bend the ball's path around his opponents. The midfielder angles his kick so the ball zooms toward one side of the net and then swerves to the other. This feat of soccer magic leaves goalies sprawled on the field. Goal!

THIS

DAVID ROBINSON OF THE SAN ANTONIO SPURS ACHIEVED A QUADRUPLE-DOUBLE ON FEBRUARY 17, 1994.

ACHIEVE A QUADRUPLE-DOUBLE

- one of the rarest feats in basketball
- achieved by getting double-digit figures in four statistics in one game
- has happened four times in NBA history

To achieve a quadruple-double, a player must dominate both ends of the court. In a single game, the player has to reach double digits in four of five categories: points, rebounds, assists, steals, and blocked shots. The first recorded quadruple-double in the NBA occurred in 1974. The Chicago Bulls' Nate Thurmond reached 22 points, 14 rebounds, 13 assists, and 12 blocked shots. Before 1973, the NBA didn't keep track of blocks and steals. It's likely that legends such as Wilt Chamberlain and Bill Russell achieved quadruple-doubles as well.

OR THAT?

HIT FOR THE NATURAL CYCLE

- one of the rarest feats in baseball
- achieved by hitting a single, double, triple, and home run, in that order, in one game
- 14 in the history of MLB

GARY MATTHEWS JR. EARNED A NATURAL CYCLE FOR THE TEXAS RANGERS ON SEPTEMBER 13, 2006.

Achieving a natural cycle seems like a supernatural feat. After nabbing a single and double, a player must hit a triple. Triples require both batter speed and a good location of the hit. But the player also needs a mighty swing to smash a home run. Bill Collins of the Boston Braves was the first to hit for the natural cycle in 1910. In 1932 Tony Lazzeri became the only player to have a natural cycle completed with a grand slam.

THIS
PLAY
PRO FOOTBALL IN THE 1920s

- centered around a few teams in the Midwest and Northeast
- helmets offered little protection
- considered less popular than college football

When football players suited up for a game in the 1920s, they looked a lot different than today's armor-clad athletes. The uniforms did not have bright colors or flashy logos. Helmets weren't required, and they were made of leather with no face masks. Shoulder pads were made of cotton covered with thick leather. With the equipment providing little protection, players suffered broken noses, broken bones, and concussions.

OR THAT?

PLAY PRO HOCKEY IN THE 1950s

- six teams
- helmet use was rare
- hockey was first being broadcast on TV

In the 1950s the NHL was made up of only six teams. The slap shot became popular during this time period. The powerful new shot added risk to the game because most players did not wear helmets. Even goalies faced the puck without a mask. In 1959 a slap shot hit Montreal Canadiens' goaltender Jacques Plante in the face, breaking his nose. He refused to go back out on the ice without a face mask. Soon more goalies joined Plante in wearing protective masks.

THIS

RICKEY HENDERSON

- MLB player, 1979–2003
- set MLB record with 1,406 career stolen bases
- stolen bases success rate: 81 percent

In the world of stolen bases, Rickey Henderson was the king of thieves. Henderson beat catchers' throws with lightning-quick running and headfirst dives. He holds the record for the most stolen bases in a career by a landslide. In far second is Lou Brock, who retired with 938 steals. Henderson is also second on the records list for single-season steals with 130 in 1982. No current player even comes close to Henderson's numbers. The base-stealing bandit entered the National Baseball Hall of Fame in 2009.

or THAT?

RETURN KICKOFFS AND PUNTS LIKE
DEVIN HESTER

- NFL player, 2006–present
- 16 career returns for a touchdown through 2011
- total career yards: 2,361 (punts); 3,126 (kickoffs)

Devin Hester is a special teams' superstar. He darts down the field on kickoff returns and dodges defenders during punt returns. In 2007 he became the first player in NFL history to run back the opening kickoff of a Super Bowl for a touchdown. At the end of the 2011 season, Hester had returned 11 punts and five kickoffs for touchdowns, an NFL record.

LIGHTNING ROUND:

☆ Score the WINNING GOAL OF THE STANLEY CUP or block your OPPONENT'S SHOT TO PREVENT THE WINNING GOAL?

☆ Hold the record for HIGHEST POLE VAULT or the FARTHEST LONG JUMP?

☆ Win an Olympic gold medal in SPEED SKATING or FIGURE SKATING?

☆ Play with your LEAST FAVORITE TEAM and WIN A CHAMPIONSHIP or play with your FAVORITE TEAM but NEVER WIN?

☆ Participate in the longest TENNIS VOLLEY or the longest VOLLEYBALL VOLLEY?

☆ Win the game by NAILING A HALF-COURT SHOT AT THE BUZZER or by KICKING A 50-YARD FIELD GOAL AS THE CLOCK RUNS OUT?

☆ Be the YOUNGEST or OLDEST professional player in a sport?

☆ Have to RUN ALL DAY in full FOOTBALL GEAR or SKATE ALL DAY in full HOCKEY GEAR?

☆ Play a game of FOOTBALL WITH ONE ARM TIED BEHIND YOUR BACK or a game of BASKETBALL ON ONE LEG?

☆ Win the KENTUCKY DERBY or the DAYTONA 500?

☆ Complete a MARATHON (26.2 MILES; 42 KM) ON A POGO STICK or BIKE A CENTURY (100 MILES; 161 KM) ON A TRICYCLE?

☆ Play a soccer game on the HOTTEST or COLDEST day of the year?

☆ Be a REFEREE IN THE NBA or an UMPIRE IN THE MLB?

☆ Be on the Olympic PING-PONG or BADMINTON team?

☆ Snowboard down MOUNT EVEREST or surf on a TSUNAMI?

☆ Have an AMAZING BACKHAND or a KILLER SERVE in tennis?

☆ Throw a GAME-WINNING TOUCHDOWN PASS or INTERCEPT THE BALL TO WIN THE GAME?

☆ Sink 60 FREE THROWS IN A ROW or swoosh 20 STRAIGHT 3-POINTERS?

☆ Get CHECKED INTO THE BOARDS IN A HOCKEY GAME or endure AN OPEN-FIELD TACKLE IN A FOOTBALL GAME?

☆ As a famous athlete, have a STREET NAMED AFTER YOU or a STATUE BUILT IN YOUR HONOR?

☆ Be a professional NASCAR DRIVER or MOTORCYCLE RACER?

☆ Correctly pick every winner in the NCAA BRACKET IN MARCH MADNESS or watch the NCAA TOURNAMENT IN PERSON?

☆ Be a SPORTS ANNOUNCER ON TELEVISION or a SPORTSWRITER FOR A NEWSPAPER?

READ MORE

Berman, Len. *The Greatest Moments in Sports.* Naperville, Ill.: Sourcebooks, 2009.

Gilpin, Daniel. *Record-Breaking People.* Record Breakers. New York: PowerKids Press, 2012.

Hurley, Michael. *Great Olympic Moments.* The Olympics. Chicago: Heinemann Library, 2012.

LeBoutillier, Nate. *The Best of Everything Baseball Book.* The All-Time Best of Sports. Mankato, Minn.: Capstone Press, 2011.

INTERNET SITES

FactHound offers a safe, fun way to find Internet sites related to this book. All of the sites on FactHound have been researched by our staff.

Here's all you do:

Visit *www.facthound.com*

Type in this code: 9781429685924

Super-cool stuff!

Check out projects, games and lots more at
www.capstonekids.com